W9-BWD-622

Matter

Cody Crane

Content Consultant

Elizabeth Case DeSantis, M.A. Elementary Education

Julia A. Stark Elementary School, Stamford, Connecticut

Reading Consultant

Jeanne M. Clidas, Ph.D.

Reading Specialist

Children's Press®

An Imprint of Scholastic Inc.

Library of Congress Cataloging-in-Publication Data
Names: Crane, Cody, author.
Title: Matter/by Cody Crane.
Other titles: Rookie read-about science.
Description: New York, NY: Children's Press,
an imprint of Scholastic Inc.,
[2019] | Series: Rookie read-about science | Includes index.
Identifiers: LCCN 2018027645| ISBN 9780531134092 (library
binding) | ISBN 9780531138038 (pbk.)
Subjects: LCSH: Matter—Properties—Juvenile literature.
Classification: LCC QC173.16 .C73 2019 | DDC 530.4—dc23

Produced by Spooky Cheetah Press
Design: Brenda Jackson
Digital Imaging: Bianca Alexis
Creative Direction: Judith E. Christ for Scholastic Inc.
© 2019 by Scholastic Inc. All rights reserved.

Published in 2019 by Children's Press, an imprint of
Scholastic Inc.

Printed in Heshan, China 62

SCHOLASTIC, CHILDREN'S PRESS, ROOKIE READ ABOUT®,
and associated logos are trademarks and/or registered
trademarks of Scholastic Inc., 557 Broadway, New York,
NY 10012.

1 2 3 4 5 6 7 8 9 10 R 28 27 26 25 24 23 22 21 20 19

Scholastic Inc., 557 Broadway, New York,
NY 10012

Photographs ©:cover main: yevgeniy11/Shutterstock;
cover background: Triff/Shutterstock; back cover: Matthias
Clamer/Stone/Getty Images; 2-3: Hal_P/Shutterstock;
5: LWA/The Image Bank/Getty Images; 6-7 background:
Yulia Buchatskaya/Shutterstock; 6 right-7 left: Eric Isselee/
Shutterstock; 7 bottom right: WendellandCarolyn/iStock;
7 bottom center: Sbolotova/Shutterstock; 9 top left: Richard
Freeda/Aurora/Getty Images; 9 top right: hanapon1002/
Shutterstock; 9 bottom: Rohappy/Dreamstime; 10: Matthias
Clamer/Stone/Getty Images; 13: Peter Cade/The Image
Bank/Getty Images; 15: Leon Neal/AFP/Getty Images;
17: Brian Bielmann/AFP/Getty Images; 18: Susan Schmitz/
Shutterstock; 19: tanuha2001/Shutterstock; 21: Mark Deibert
Productions/Shutterstock; 22: pisaphotography/Shutterstock;
25 main: baona/E+/Getty Images; 25 cloud: grafikwork/
Shutterstock; 27: Soft_Light/iStockphoto; 28: AbbieImages/
StockFood Creative/Getty Images; 29: AfriPics.com/Alamy
Images; 30 top: hanapon1002/Shutterstock; 30 center:
Rohappy/Dreamstime; 30 bottom: tanuha2001/Shutterstock;
31 top: Leon Neal/AFP/Getty Images; 31 bottom: Matthias
Clamer/Stone/Getty Images; 31 center: Richard Freeda/
Aurora/Getty Images; 32: Bernard van Dierendonck/LOOK/
Getty Images.

Table of Contents

Chapter 1

What Is Matter?

Everything on Earth is made up of matter. These kids are playing at the beach. They are made up of matter. The ocean, the sand, and even the air around them are made up of matter, too.

5

Matter is anything that takes up space. Everything you can see, feel, touch, or smell is made of matter.

Which dog is bigger?

Does the bigger dog have more matter?

There are three main types, or **states**, of matter. Each of them looks and acts in a different way.

Is it easy to change a rock's shape?

What happens to the water as the girl tips the bottle?

What is inside those bubbles?

solid

liquid

gas

9

10

Chapter 2

What Are Solids?

Solid matter has its own shape. Its shape is not easy to change.

If a solid's shape changes,
it is hard to make it look
how it did before.

Can you
fix the lamp
so it looks just
like it did
before?

13

You can use a **scale** to measure how much a solid weighs. The more matter there is in a solid, the heavier it will be.

Which weighs more: you or a toad?

15

Chapter 3

What Are Liquids?

Liquid matter does not hold its shape like a solid does. It is able to **flow**. Water is a liquid. It is able to move around this surfer.

17

A liquid does not keep its shape because it moves easily. It takes the shape of whatever container it is in.

How do we keep liquids in one place?

19

You can use a measuring cup to measure liquids. That is how you know the right amount of milk to add to a cake recipe.

How much milk will it take to fill the measuring cup?

21

What Are Gases?

A **gas** spreads out to fill the space it is in. That means its shape can change.

Clouds are made of gas.
The air you breathe is a mixture
of gases, too. Gases are all
around us even though we
cannot see them.

What shape did this cloud take?

25

Visible or invisible, big or small, broken or whole, everything around you is made up of matter.

Can you spot all three types of matter in this photo?

Changing Matter

Can you change matter's state?

Remember to ask an adult for help with this activity.

1. Take an ice cube out of the freezer. Place it inside a cup. Let it melt.

2. Pour the water into a sandwich bag and place it in the freezer until ice forms again.

What Happened?

Heating matter can change its state. As an ice cube warms up outside the freezer, it melts into water. It changes from solid matter to liquid matter. Cooling the water in the freezer changes its state again. The liquid matter turns again into solid matter. The ice takes the shape of the container holding it.

flow (floh): to move in a stream

- *The water in the bottle* **flows** *into the girl's mouth.*

gas (gass): a type of matter that spreads out to fill the space it is in

- *A bubble forms as it is filled with* **gas**.

liquid (**lih**-kwid): a type of matter that flows to take the shape of whatever it is in

- *The* **liquid** *in this fishbowl takes the shape of the bowl.*

scale (skayl): a tool used to weigh solid objects

- *The **scale** measures how heavy the toad is.*

---

solid (**sah**-lid): a type of matter that keeps its shape

- *It is hard to change the shape of a rock because it is a **solid**.*

---

states (stayts): the three forms of matter

- *A solid is an example of one **state** of matter.*

Index

Facts for Now

Visit this
Scholastic website
for more information on
matter, and to download
the Reader's
Guide for this series:
**http://www.factsfornow.
scholastic.com**
Enter the keyword
Matter

About the Author

Cody Crane
is an award-winning
children's science
writer. She lives in Texas
with her husband
and son.